TEACHING
SMART PEOPLE
HOW TO LEARN

HARVARD BUSINESS REVIEW
CLASSICS

TEACHING
SMART PEOPLE
HOW TO LEARN

Chris Argyris

Harvard Business Review Press
Boston, Massachusetts

Library of Congress Cataloging-in-Publication Data
Argyris, Chris, 1923-
  Teaching smart people how to learn / Chris Argyris.
    p. cm. – (The Harvard business review classics series)
  "Reprint 4304"–T.P. verso.
  Reprint of an article previously published in the Harvard business
review.
  ISBN 978-1-4221-2600-4 (pbk. : alk. paper) 1. Organizational
learning--Psychological aspects. 2. Defensiveness (Psychology)
3. Self-evaluation. 4. Active learning. 5. Organizational effective-
ness. I. Harvard business review. II. Title.
  HD58.82.A739 2008
  658.3′124–dc22

                                              2008005632

THE
HARVARD BUSINESS REVIEW
CLASSICS SERIES

Since 1922, *Harvard Business Review* has
been a leading source of breakthrough ideas
in management practice—many of which still
speak to and influence us today. The HBR
Classics series now offers you the opportunity
to make these seminal pieces a part of your
permanent management library. Each vol-
ume contains a groundbreaking idea that has
shaped best practices and inspired countless
managers around the world—and will change
how you think about the business world today.

TEACHING
SMART PEOPLE
HOW TO LEARN

Any company that aspires to succeed in the tougher business environment of the 1990s must first resolve a basic dilemma: success in the marketplace increasingly depends on learning, yet most people don't know how to learn. What's more, those members of the organization that many assume to be the best at learning are, in fact, not very good at it. I am talking about the well-educated, high-powered, high-commitment professionals who occupy key leadership positions in the modern corporation.

Most companies not only have tremendous difficulty addressing this learning dilemma; they aren't even aware that it exists. The reason: they misunderstand what learning is and how to bring it about. As a result, they tend to make two mistakes in their efforts to become a learning organization.

First, most people define learning too narrowly as mere "problem solving," so they focus on identifying and correcting errors in the external environment. Solving problems is important. But if learning is to persist, managers and employees must also look inward. They need to reflect critically on their own behavior, identify the ways they often inadvertently contribute to the organization's problems, and then change how they act. In particular, they must learn how the very way they go about defining and solving problems can be a source of problems in its own right.

I have coined the terms "single loop" and "double loop" learning to capture this crucial distinction. To give a simple analogy: a thermostat that automatically turns on the heat whenever the temperature in a room drops below 68 degrees is a good example of single-loop learning. A thermostat that could ask, "Why am I set at 68 degrees?" and then explore whether or not some other temperature might more economically achieve the goal of heating the room would be engaging in double-loop learning.

Highly skilled professionals are frequently very good at single-loop learning. After all, they have spent much of their lives acquiring academic credentials, mastering one or a number of intellectual disciplines, and applying those disciplines to solve real-world problems. But ironically, this very fact helps explain why professionals are often so bad at double-loop learning.

Put simply, because many professionals are almost always successful at what they do, they rarely experience failure. And because they have rarely failed, they have never learned how to learn from failure. So whenever their single-loop learning strategies go wrong, they become defensive, screen out criticism, and put the "blame" on anyone and everyone but themselves. In short, their ability to learn shuts down precisely at the moment they need it the most.

The propensity among professionals to behave defensively helps shed light on the second mistake that companies make about learning. The common assumption is that getting people to learn is largely a matter of motivation. When people have the right attitudes and commitment, learning automatically follows. So companies focus on creating new organizational structures—compensation programs, performance reviews, corporate cultures, and the like—that are designed to create motivated and committed employees.

But effective double-loop learning is not simply a function of how people feel. It is a reflection of how they think—that is, the cognitive rules or reasoning they use to design and implement their actions. Think of these rules as a kind of "master program" stored in the brain, governing all behavior. Defensive reasoning can block learning even when the individual commitment to it is high, just as a computer program with hidden bugs can produce results exactly the opposite of what its designers had planned.

Companies can learn how to resolve the learning dilemma. What it takes is to make the ways managers and employees reason about their behavior a focus of organizational learning and continuous improvement programs. Teaching people how to reason about their behavior in new and more effective ways breaks down the defenses that block learning.

All of the examples that follow involve a particular kind of professional: fast-track consultants at major management consulting companies. But the implications of my argument go far beyond this specific occupational group. The fact is, more and more jobs—no matter what the title—are taking on the contours of "knowledge work." People at all levels of the organization must combine the mastery of some highly specialized technical expertise with the ability to work effectively in teams, form productive relationships with clients and customers, and critically reflect on and then change their own organizational practices. And the nuts and bolts of management—whether of high-powered consultants or service representatives, senior managers or factory technicians—increasingly consists of guiding and integrating the autonomous

but interconnected work of highly skilled
people.

HOW PROFESSIONALS AVOID LEARNING

For 15 years, I have been conducting in-
depth studies of management consultants. I
decided to study consultants for a few simple
reasons. First, they are the epitome of the
highly educated professionals who play an increasingly central role in all organizations.
Almost all of the consultants I've studied have
MBAs from the top three or four U.S. business schools. They are also highly committed
to their work. For instance, at one company,
more than 90% of the consultants responded

in a survey that they were "highly satisfied" with their jobs and with the company.

I also assumed that such professional consultants would be good at learning. After all, the essence of their job is to teach others how to do things differently. I found, however, that these consultants embodied the learning dilemma. The most enthusiastic about continuous improvement in their own organizations, they were also often the biggest obstacle to its complete success.

As long as efforts at learning and change focused on external organizational factors—job redesign, compensation programs, performance reviews, and leadership training—the professionals were enthusiastic participants. Indeed, creating new systems and structures was precisely the kind of challenge that well-educated, highly motivated professionals thrived on.

And yet the moment the quest for continuous improvement turned to the professionals' *own* performance, something went wrong. It wasn't a matter of bad attitude. The professionals' commitment to excellence was genuine, and the vision of the company was clear. Nevertheless, continuous improvement did not persist. And the longer the continuous improvement efforts continued, the greater the likelihood that they would produce ever-diminishing returns.

What happened? The professionals began to feel embarrassed. They were threatened by the prospect of critically examining their own role in the organization. Indeed, because they were so well paid (and generally believed that their employers were supportive and fair), the idea that their performance might not be at its best made them feel guilty.

Far from being a catalyst for real change, such feelings caused most to react defensively. They projected the blame for any problems away from themselves and onto what they said were unclear goals, insensitive and unfair leaders, and stupid clients.

Consider this example. At a premier management consulting company, the manager of a case team called a meeting to examine the team's performance on a recent consulting project. The client was largely satisfied and had given the team relatively high marks, but the manager believed the team had not created the value added that it was capable of and that the consulting company had promised. In the spirit of continuous improvement, he felt that the team could do better. Indeed, so did some of the team members.

The manager knew how difficult it was for people to reflect critically on their own work performance, especially in the presence of their manager, so he took a number of steps to make possible a frank and open discussion. He invited to the meeting an outside consultant whom team members knew and trusted—"just to keep me honest," he said. He also agreed to have the entire meeting tape-recorded. That way, any subsequent confusions or disagreements about what went on at the meeting could be checked against the transcript. Finally, the manager opened the meeting by emphasizing that no subject was off limits—including his own behavior.

"I realize that you may believe you cannot confront me," the manager said. "But I encourage you to challenge me. You have a responsibility to tell me where you think the leadership made mistakes, just as I have the responsibility to identify any I believe you made. And all of us must acknowledge our own mistakes. If we do not have an open dialogue, we will not learn."

The professionals took the manager up on the first half of his invitation but quietly ignored the second. When asked to pinpoint the key problems in the experience with the client, they looked entirely outside themselves. The clients were uncooperative and arrogant. "They didn't think we could help them." The team's own managers were unavailable and poorly prepared. "At times, our managers were not up to speed before they walked into the client meetings." In effect, the professionals asserted that they were helpless to act differently—not because of any limitations of their own but because of the limitations of others.

The manager listened carefully to the team members and tried to respond to their criticisms. He talked about the mistakes that he had made during the consulting process. For example, one professional objected to

the way the manager had run the project
meetings. "I see that the way I asked ques-
tions closed down discussions," responded
the manager. "I didn't mean to do that, but
I can see how you might have believed that
I had already made up my mind." Another
team member complained that the manager
had caved in to pressure from his superior to
produce the project report far too quickly,
considering the team's heavy work load. "I
think that it was my responsibility to have
said no," admitted the manager. "It was clear
that we all had an immense amount of work."

Finally, after some three hours of discussion about his own behavior, the manager
began to ask the team members if there were
any errors *they* might have made. "After

all," he said, "this client was not different from many others. How can we be more effective in the future?"

The professionals repeated that it was really the clients' and their own managers' fault. As one put it, "They have to be open to change and want to learn." The more the manager tried to get the team to examine its own responsibility for the outcome, the more the professionals bypassed his concerns. The best one team member could suggest was for the case team to "promise less"—implying that there was really no way for the group to improve its performance.

The case team members were reacting defensively to protect themselves, even though their manager was not acting in ways that an outsider would consider threatening. Even if there were some truth to their charges—the clients may well have been arrogant and closed, their own managers distant—the way they presented these claims was guaranteed to stop learning. With few exceptions, the professionals made attributions about the behavior of the clients and the managers but never publicly tested their claims. For instance, they said that the clients weren't motivated to learn but never really presented any evidence supporting that assertion. When their lack of concrete evidence was pointed out to them, they simply repeated their criticisms more vehemently.

If the professionals had felt so strongly about these issues, why had they never mentioned them during the project? According to the professionals, even this was the fault of others. "We didn't want to alienate the client," argued one. "We didn't want to be seen as whining," said another.

The professionals were using their criticisms of others to protect themselves from the potential embarrassment of having to admit that perhaps they too had contributed to the team's less-than-perfect performance. What's more, the fact that they kept repeating their defensive actions in the face of the manager's efforts to turn the group's attention to its own role shows that this defensiveness had become a reflexive routine. From the professionals' perspective, they weren't resisting; they were focusing on the "real" causes. Indeed, they were to be respected, if not congratulated, for working as well as they did under such difficult conditions.

The end result was an unproductive parallel conversation. Both the manager and the professionals were candid; they expressed their views forcefully. But they talked past each other, never finding a common language to describe what had happened with the client. The professionals kept insisting that the fault lay with others. The manager kept trying, unsuccessfully, to get the professionals to see how they contributed to the state of affairs they were criticizing. The dialogue of this parallel conversation looks like this:

Professionals: "The clients have to be open. They must want to change."

Manager: "It's our task to help them see that change is in their interest."

{ 19 }

Professionals: "But the clients didn't agree with our analyses."

Manager: "If they didn't think our ideas were right, how might we have convinced them?"

Professionals: "Maybe we need to have more meetings with the client."

Manager: "If we aren't adequately prepared and if the clients don't think we're credible, how will more meetings help?"

Professionals: "There should be better communication between case team members and management."

Manager: "I agree. But professionals should take the initiative to educate the manager about the problems they are experiencing."

Professionals: "Our leaders are unavailable and distant."

Manager: "How do you expect us to know that if you don't tell us?"

Conversations such as this one dramatically illustrate the learning dilemma. The problem with the professionals' claims is not that they are wrong but that they aren't useful. By constantly turning the focus away from their own behavior to that of others, the professionals bring learning to a grinding halt. The manager understands the trap but does not know how to get out of it. To learn how to do that requires going deeper into the dynamics of defensive reasoning—and into the special causes that make professionals so prone to it.

DEFENSIVE REASONING AND THE DOOM LOOP

What explains the professionals' defensiveness? Not their attitudes about change or commitment to continuous improvement; they really wanted to work more effectively. Rather, the key factor is the way they reasoned about their behavior and that of others.

It is impossible to reason anew in every situation. If we had to think through all the possible responses every time someone asked, "How are you?" the world would pass us by. Therefore, everyone develops a theory of action—a set of rules that individuals use to design and implement their own behavior as well as to understand the behavior of others. Usually, these theories of actions become so taken for granted that people don't even realize they are using them.

One of the paradoxes of human behavior, however, is that the master program people actually use is rarely the one they think they use. Ask people in an interview or questionnaire to articulate the rules they use to govern their actions, and they will give you what I call their "espoused" theory of action. But observe these same people's behavior, and you will quickly see that this espoused theory has very little to do with how they actually behave. For example, the professionals on the case team said they believed in continuous improvement, and yet they consistently acted in ways that made improvement impossible.

When you observe people's behavior and try to come up with rules that would make sense of it, you discover a very different theory of action—what I call the individual's "theory-in-use." Put simply, people consistently act inconsistently, unaware of the contradiction between their espoused theory and their theory-in-use, between the way they think they are acting and the way they really act.

What's more, most theories-in-use rest on the same set of governing values. There seems to be a universal human tendency to design one's actions consistently according to four basic values:

1. To remain in unilateral control;

2. To maximize "winning" and minimize "losing";

3. To suppress negative feelings; and

4. To be as "rational" as possible—by which people mean defining clear objectives and evaluating their behavior in terms of whether or not they have achieved them.

The purpose of all these values is to avoid embarrassment or threat, feeling vulnerable or incompetent. In this respect, the master program that most people use is profoundly defensive. Defensive reasoning encourages individuals to keep private the premises, inferences, and conclusions that shape their behavior and to avoid testing them in a truly independent, objective fashion.

Because the attributions that go into defensive reasoning are never really tested, it is a closed loop, remarkably impervious to conflicting points of view. The inevitable response to the observation that somebody is reasoning defensively is yet more defensive reasoning. With the case team, for example, whenever anyone pointed out the professionals' defensive behavior to them, their initial reaction was to look for the cause in somebody else—clients who were so sensitive that they would have been alienated if the consultants had criticized them or a manager so weak that he couldn't have taken it had the consultants raised their concerns with him. In other words, the case team members once again denied their own responsibility by externalizing the problem and putting it on someone else.

In such situations, the simple act of encouraging more open inquiry is often attacked by others as "intimidating." Those who do the attacking deal with their feelings about possibly being wrong by blaming the more open individual for arousing these feelings and upsetting them.

Needless to say, such a master program inevitably short-circuits learning. And for a number of reasons unique to their psychology, well-educated professionals are especially susceptible to this.

Nearly all the consultants I have studied have stellar academic records. Ironically, their very success at education helps explain the problems they have with learning. Before they enter the world of work, their lives are primarily full of successes, so they have rarely experienced the embarrassment and sense of threat that comes with failure. As a result, their defensive reasoning has rarely been activated. People who rarely experience failure, however, end up not knowing how to deal with it effectively. And this serves to reinforce the normal human tendency to reason defensively.

In a survey of several hundred young consultants at the organizations I have been studying, these professionals describe themselves as driven internally by an unrealistically high ideal of performance: "Pressure on the job is self-imposed." "I must not only do a good job; I must also be the best." "People around here are very bright and hardworking; they are highly motivated to do an outstanding job." "Most of us want not only to succeed but also to do so at maximum speed."

These consultants are always comparing themselves with the best around them and constantly trying to better their own performance. And yet they do not appreciate being required to compete openly with each other. They feel it is somehow inhumane.

They prefer to be the individual contributor— what might be termed a "productive loner."

Behind this high aspiration for success is an equally high fear of failure and a propensity to feel shame and guilt when they do fail to meet their high standards. "You must avoid mistakes," said one. "I hate making them. Many of us fear failure, whether we admit it or not."

To the extent that these consultants have experienced success in their lives, they have not had to be concerned about failure and the attendant feelings of shame and guilt. But to exactly the same extent, they also have never developed the tolerance for feelings of failure or the skills to deal with these feelings. This in turn has led them not only to fear failure but also to fear the fear of failure itself. For they know that they will not cope with it superlatively—their usual level of aspiration.

The consultants use two intriguing metaphors to describe this phenomenon. They talk about the "doom loop" and "doom zoom." Often, consultants will perform well on the case team, but because they don't do the jobs perfectly or receive accolades from their managers, they go into a doom loop of despair. And they don't ease into the doom loop, they zoom into it.

As a result, many professionals have extremely "brittle" personalities. When suddenly faced with a situation they cannot immediately handle, they tend to fall apart. They cover up their distress in front of the client. They talk about it constantly with their fellow case team members. Interestingly, these conversations commonly take the form of bad-mouthing clients.

Such brittleness leads to an inappropriately high sense of despondency or even despair when people don't achieve the high levels of performance they aspire to. Such despondency is rarely psychologically devastating, but when combined with defensive reasoning, it can result in a formidable predisposition against learning.

There is no better example of how this brittleness can disrupt an organization than performance evaluations. Because it represents the one moment when a professional must measure his or her own behavior against some formal standard, a performance evaluation is almost tailor-made to push a professional into the doom loop. Indeed, a poor evaluation can reverberate far beyond the particular individual involved to spark defensive reasoning throughout an entire organization.

At one consulting company, management established a new performance-evaluation process that was designed to make evaluations both more objective and more useful to those being evaluated. The consultants participated in the design of the new system and in general were enthusiastic because it corresponded to their espoused values of objectivity and fairness. A brief two years into the new process, however, it had become the object of dissatisfaction. The catalyst for this about-face was the first unsatisfactory rating.

Senior managers had identified six consultants whose performance they considered below standard. In keeping with the new evaluation process, they did all they could to communicate their concerns to the six and to help them improve. Managers met with each individual separately for as long and as often as the professional requested to explain the reasons behind the rating and to discuss what needed to be done to improve—but to no avail. Performance continued at the same low level and, eventually, the six were let go.

When word of the dismissal spread through the company, people responded with confusion and anxiety. After about a dozen consultants angrily complained to management, the CEO held two lengthy meetings where employees could air their concerns.

At the meetings, the professionals made a variety of claims. Some said the perform- ance-evaluation process was unfair because judgments were subjective and biased and the criteria for minimum performance un- clear. Others suspected that the real cause for the dismissals was economic and that the performance-evaluation procedure was just a fig leaf to hide the fact that the company was in trouble. Still others argued that the evalu- ation process was antilearning. If the com- pany were truly a learning organization, as it claimed, then people performing below the minimum standard should be taught how to reach it. As one professional put it: "We were told that the company did not have an up-or-out policy. Up-or-out is inconsistent with learning. You misled us."

The CEO tried to explain the logic behind management's decision by grounding it in the facts of the case and by asking the professionals for any evidence that might contradict these facts.

Is there subjectivity and bias in the evaluation process? Yes, responded the CEO, but "we strive hard to reduce them. We are constantly trying to improve the process. If you have any ideas, please tell us. If you know of someone treated unfairly, please bring it up. If any of you feel that you have been treated unfairly, let's discuss it now or, if you wish, privately."

Is the level of minimum competence too vague? "We are working to define minimum competence more clearly," he answered. "In the case of the six, however, their performance was so poor that it wasn't difficult to reach a decision." Most of the six had received timely feedback about their problems. And in the two cases where people had not, the reason was that they had never taken the responsibility to seek out evaluations—and, indeed, had actively avoided them. "If you have any data to the contrary," the CEO added, "let's talk about it."

Were the six asked to leave for economic reasons? No, said the CEO. "We have more work than we can do, and letting professionals go is extremely costly for us. Do any of you have any information to the contrary?"

As to the company being antilearning, in fact, the entire evaluation process was designed to encourage learning. When a professional is performing below the minimum level, the CEO explained, "we jointly design remedial experiences with the individual. Then we look for signs of improvement. In these cases, either the professionals were reluctant to take on such assignments or they repeatedly failed when they did. Again, if you have information or evidence to the contrary, I'd like to hear about it."

The CEO concluded: "It's regrettable, but sometimes we make mistakes and hire

the wrong people. If individuals don't produce and repeatedly prove themselves unable to improve, we don't know what else to
do except dismiss them. It's just not fair to
keep poorly performing individuals in the
company. They earn an unfair share of the
financial rewards."

Instead of responding with data of their
own, the professionals simply repeated their
accusations but in ways that consistently
contradicted their claims. They said that a
genuinely fair evaluation process would con-
tain clear and documentable data about performance—but they were unable to provide
firsthand examples of the unfairness that
they implied colored the evaluation of the
six dismissed employees. They argued that

people shouldn't be judged by inferences unconnected to their actual performance—but they judged management in precisely this way. They insisted that management define clear, objective, and unambiguous performance standards—but they argued that any humane system would take into account that the performance of a professional cannot be precisely measured. Finally, they presented themselves as champions of learning—but they never proposed any criteria for assessing whether an individual might be unable to learn.

In short, the professionals seemed to hold management to a different level of performance than they held themselves. In their conversation at the meetings, they used many of

the features of ineffective evaluation that
they condemned—the absence of concrete
data, for example, and the dependence on a
circular logic of "heads we win, tails you
lose." It is as if they were saying, "Here are
the features of a fair performance-evaluation
system. You should abide by them. But we
don't have to when we are evaluating you."

Indeed, if we were to explain the professionals' behavior by articulating rules that
would have to be in their heads in order for
them to act the way they did, the rules would
look something like this:

1. When criticizing the company, state
   your criticism in ways that you believe
   are valid—but also in ways that prevent

others from deciding for themselves whether your claim to validity is correct.

2. When asked to illustrate your criticisms, don't include any data that others could use to decide for themselves whether the illustrations are valid.

3. State your conclusions in ways that disguise their logical implications. If others point out those implications to you, deny them.

Of course, when such rules were described to the professionals, they found them abhorrent. It was inconceivable that these rules might explain their actions. And yet in defending themselves against this observation,

they almost always inadvertently confirmed
the rules.

LEARNING HOW TO REASON
PRODUCTIVELY

If defensive reasoning is as widespread as I
believe, then focusing on an individual's attitudes or commitment is never enough to
produce real change. And as the previous
example illustrates, neither is creating new
organizational structures or systems. The
problem is that even when people are genuinely committed to improving their performance and management has changed its
structures in order to encourage the "right"
kind of behavior, people still remain locked

in defensive reasoning. Either they remain unaware of this fact, or if they do become aware of it, they blame others.

There is, however, reason to believe that organizations can break out of this vicious circle. Despite the strength of defensive reasoning, people genuinely strive to produce what they intend. They value acting competently. Their self-esteem is intimately tied up with behaving consistently and performing effectively. Companies can use these universal human tendencies to teach people how to reason in a new way—in effect, to change the master programs in their heads and thus reshape their behavior.

People can be taught how to recognize the reasoning they use when they design and im-

plement their actions. They can begin to
identify the inconsistencies between their
espoused and actual theories of action. They
can face up to the fact that they uncon-
sciously design and implement actions that
they do not intend. Finally, people can learn
how to identify what individuals and groups
do to create organizational defenses and how
these defenses contribute to an organization's
problems.

Once companies embark on this learning
process, they will discover that the kind of
reasoning necessary to reduce and overcome
organizational defenses is the same kind of
"tough reasoning" that underlies the effective use of ideas in strategy, finance, market-
ing, manufacturing, and other management

disciplines. Any sophisticated strategic analysis, for example, depends on collecting valid data, analyzing it carefully, and constantly testing the inferences drawn from the data. The toughest tests are reserved for the conclusions. Good strategists make sure that their conclusions can withstand all kinds of critical questioning.

So too with productive reasoning about human behavior. The standard of analysis is just as high. Human resource programs no longer need to be based on "soft" reasoning but should be as analytical and as data-driven as any other management discipline.

Of course, that is not the kind of reasoning the consultants used when they encountered problems that were embarrassing or threatening. The data they collected was hardly objective. The inferences they made rarely became explicit. The conclusions they reached were largely self-serving, impossible for others to test, and as a result, "self-sealing," impervious to change.

How can an organization begin to turn this situation around, to teach its members how to reason productively? The first step is for managers at the top to examine critically and change their own theories-in-use. Until senior managers become aware of how they reason defensively and the counterproductive consequences that result, there will be little real progress. Any change activity is likely to be just a fad.

Change has to start at the top because otherwise defensive senior managers are likely to disown any transformation in reasoning patterns coming from below. If professionals or middle managers begin to change the way they reason and act, such changes are likely to appear strange—if not actually dangerous—to those at the top. The result is an unstable situation where senior managers still believe that it is a sign of caring and sensitivity to bypass and cover up difficult issues, while their subordinates see the very same actions as defensive.

The key to any educational experience designed to teach senior managers how to reason productively is to connect the program to real business problems. The best demonstration of the usefulness of productive reasoning is for busy managers to see how it can make a direct difference in their own performance and in that of the organization. This will not happen overnight. Managers need plenty of opportunity to practice the new skills. But once they grasp the powerful impact that productive reasoning can have on actual performance, they will have a strong incentive to reason productively not just in a training session but in all their work relationships.

One simple approach I have used to get this process started is to have participants produce a kind of rudimentary case study. The subject is a real business problem that the manager either wants to deal with or has tried unsuccessfully to address in the past. Writing the actual case usually takes less than an hour. But then the case becomes the focal point of an extended analysis.

For example, a CEO at a large organizational-development consulting company was pre-occupied with the problems caused by the intense competition among the various business functions represented by his four direct reports. Not only was he tired of having the problems dumped in his lap, but he was also worried about the impact the interfunctional conflicts were having on the organization's flexibility. He had even calculated that the money being spent to iron out disagreements amounted to hundreds of thousands of dollars every year. And the more fights there were, the more defensive people became, which only increased the costs to the organization.

In a paragraph or so, the CEO described a meeting he intended to have with his direct reports to address the problem. Next, he divided the paper in half, and on the right-hand side of the page, he wrote a scenario for the meeting—much like the script for a movie or play—describing what he would say and how his subordinates would likely respond. On the left-hand side of the page, he wrote down any thoughts and feelings that he would be likely to have during the meeting but that he wouldn't express for fear they would derail the discussion.

But instead of holding the meeting, the CEO analyzed this scenario *with* his direct reports. The case became the catalyst for a discussion in which the CEO learned several things about the way he acted with his management team.

He discovered that his four direct reports often perceived his conversations as counter-

Chris Argyris

productive. In the guise of being "diplomatic," he would pretend that a consensus about the problem existed, when in fact none existed. The unintended result: instead of feeling reassured, his subordinates felt wary and tried to figure out "what is he *really* getting at."

The CEO also realized that the way he dealt with the competitiveness among department heads was completely contradictory. On the one hand, he kept urging them to "think of the organization as a whole." On the other, he kept calling for actions—department budget cuts, for example—that placed them directly in competition with each other.

Finally, the CEO discovered that many of the tacit evaluations and attributions he had listed turned out to be wrong. Since he had never expressed these assumptions, he had never found out just how wrong they were. What's more, he learned that much of what he thought he was hiding came through to his subordinates anyway—but with the added message that the boss was covering up.

The CEO's colleagues also learned about their own ineffective behavior. They learned by examining their own behavior as they tried to help the CEO analyze his case. They also learned by writing and analyzing cases of their own. They began to see that they too tended to bypass and cover up the real issues and that the CEO was often aware of it but did not say so. They too made inaccurate attributions and evaluations that they did not express. Moreover, the belief that they had to hide important ideas and feelings from the CEO and from each other in order not to upset anyone turned out to be mistaken. In the context of the case discussions, the entire senior management team was quite willing to discuss what had always been undiscussable.

In effect, the case study exercise legitimizes talking about issues that people have never been able to address before. Such a discussion can be emotional—even painful. But for managers with the courage to persist, the payoff is great: management teams and entire organizations work more openly and more effectively and have greater options for behaving flexibly and adapting to particular situations.

When senior managers are trained in new reasoning skills, they can have a big impact

on the performance of the entire organization—even when other employees are still
reasoning defensively. The CEO who led the
meetings on the performance-evaluation
procedure was able to defuse dissatisfaction
because he didn't respond to professionals'
criticisms in kind but instead gave a clear
presentation of relevant data. Indeed, most
participants took the CEO's behavior to be a
sign that the company really acted on the values of participation and employee involve-
ment that it espoused.

Of course, the ideal is for all the members
of an organization to learn how to reason
productively. This has happened at the company where the case team meeting took place.
Consultants and their managers are now
able to confront some of the most difficult

issues of the consultant-client relationship. To get a sense of the difference productive reasoning can make, imagine how the original conversation between the manager and case team might have gone had everyone engaged in effective reasoning. (The following dialogue is based on actual sessions I have attended with other case teams at the same company since the training has been completed.)

First, the consultants would have demonstrated their commitment to continuous improvement by being willing to examine their own role in the difficulties that arose during the consulting project. No doubt they would have identified their managers and the clients as part of the problem, but they would have gone on to admit that they had contributed to it as well. More important, they would have agreed with the manager that as they explored the various roles of clients, managers, and professionals, they would make sure to test any evaluations or attributions they might make against the data. Each individual would have encouraged the others to question his or her reasoning. Indeed, they would have insisted on it. And in turn, everyone would have understood that act of questioning not as a sign of mistrust or an invasion of privacy but as a valuable opportunity for learning.

The conversation about the manager's unwillingness to say no might look something like this:

Professional #1: "One of the biggest problems I had with the way you managed this case was that you seemed to be unable to say no when either the client or your superior made unfair demands." [Gives an example.]

Professional #2: "I have another example to add. [Describes a second example.] But I'd also like to say that we never really told you how we felt about this. Behind your back we were bad-mouthing you— you know, 'he's being such a wimp'—but we never came right out and said it."

Manager: "It certainly would have been helpful if you had said something. Was there anything I said or did that gave you the idea that you had better not raise this with me?"

Professional #3: "Not really. I think we didn't want to sound like we were whining."

Manager: "Well, I certainly don't think you sound like you're whining. But two thoughts come to mind. If I understand you correctly, you *were* complaining, but the complaining about me and my inability to say no was covered up. Second, if we had discussed this, I might have gotten the data I needed to be able to say no."

Notice that when the second professional describes how the consultants had covered up their complaints, the manager doesn't criticize her. Rather, he rewards her for being open by responding in kind. He focuses on the ways that he too may have contributed to the cover-up. Reflecting undefensively about his own role in the problem then makes it possible for the professionals to talk about their fears of appearing to be whining. The manager then agrees with the professionals that they shouldn't become complainers. At the same time, he points out the counterproductive consequences of covering up their complaints.

Another unresolved issue in the case team meeting concerned the supposed arrogance of the clients. A more productive conversation about that problem might go like this:

Manager: "You said that the clients were arrogant and uncooperative. What did they say and do?"

Professional #1: "One asked me if I had ever met a payroll. Another asked how long I've been out of school."

Professional #2: "One even asked me how old I was!"

Professional #3: "That's nothing. The worst is when they say that all we do is interview people, write a report based on what they tell us, and then collect our fees."

Manager: "The fact that we tend to be so young is a real problem for many of our clients. They get very defensive about it.

But I'd like to explore whether there is a way for them to freely express their views without our getting defensive . . ."

"What troubled me about your original responses was that you assumed you were right in calling the clients stupid. One thing I've noticed about consultants—in this company and others—is that we tend to defend ourselves by bad-mouthing the client."

Professional #1: "Right. After all, if they are genuinely stupid, then it's obviously not our fault that they aren't getting it!"

Professional #2: "Of course, that stance is antilearning and overprotective. By assuming that they can't learn, we absolve ourselves from having to."

{ 62 }

Professional #3: "And the more we all go along with the bad-mouthing, the more we reinforce each other's defensiveness."

Manager: "So what's the alternative? How can we encourage our clients to express their defensiveness and at the same time constructively build on it?"

Professional #1: "We all know that the real issue isn't our age; it's whether or not we are able to add value to the client's organization. They should judge us by what we produce. And if we aren't adding value, they should get rid of us—no matter how young or old we happen to be."

Manager: "Perhaps that is exactly what we should tell them."

In both these examples, the consultants and their manager are doing real work. They are learning about their own group dynamics and addressing some generic problems in client-consultant relationships. The insights they gain will allow them to act more effectively in the future—both as individuals and as a team. They are not just solving problems but developing a far deeper and more textured understanding of their role as members of the organization. They are laying the groundwork for continuous improvement that is truly continuous. They are learning how to learn.

ABOUT THE AUTHOR

Chris Argyris is the James Bryant Conant Professor Emeritus of Education and Organizational Behavior at Harvard University.

ALSO BY THIS AUTHOR

***Harvard Business Review* Articles**

"Double Loop Learning in Organizations"

"Empowerment: The Emperor's New Clothes"

"Good Communication that Blocks Learning"

"Interpersonal Barriers to Decision Making"

"Skilled Incompetence"

Article Summary

The Idea at Work

People often profess to be open to critique and new learning, but their actions suggest a very different set of governing values or theories-in-use:

- the desire to remain in unilateral control

- the goal of maximizing "winning" while minimizing "losing"

- the belief that negative feelings should be suppressed

- the desire to appear as rational as possible.

Taken together, these values betray a profoundly defensive posture: a need to avoid embarrassment, threat, or feelings of vulnerability and incompetence. This closed-loop reasoning explains why the mere encouragement of open inquiry can be intimidating to some. And it's especially relevant to the behavior of many of the most highly skilled and best-trained employees. Behind their high aspirations are an equally high fear of failure and a tendency to be ashamed when they don't live up to their high standards. Consequently, they become brittle and despondent in situations in which they don't excel immediately.

Fortunately, it *is* possible for individuals and organizations to develop more productive patterns of behavior. Two suggestions for how to make this happen:

1. *Apply the same kind of "tough reasoning" you use to conduct strategic analysis.* Collect the most objective data you can find.

Make your inferences explicit and test them constantly. Submit your conclusions to the toughest tests of all: make sure they aren't self-serving or impossible for others to verify.

2. *Senior managers must model the desired changes first.* When the leadership demonstrates its willingness to examine critically its own theories-in-use, changing them as indicated, everyone will find it easier to do the same.

Example: The CEO of an organizational-development firm created a case study to address real problems caused by the intense competition among his direct reports. In a paragraph, he described a meeting he intended to have with his subordinates. Then he wrote down what he planned to say, how he thought his subordinates would respond, as well as any thoughts or feelings he thought he might have but not express for fear of derailing the conversation. Instead of actually holding the meeting, he analyzed the scenario he had developed *with* his direct reports. The result was an illuminating conversation in which the CEO and his subordinates were able to circumvent the closed-loop reasoning that had characterized so many prior discussions.

CPSIA information can be obtained
at www.ICGtesting.com
Printed in the USA
JSHW021006140723
44758JS00004B/6

9 781422 126004